Words of an Introvert

Hungchano M Kikon

BookLeaf
Publishing

India | USA | UK

Presentation by *BookLeaf Publishing*

Web: www.bookleafpub.com

E-mail: info@bookleafpub.com

ISBN: 9789360941338

First edition 2024

ACKNOWLEDGEMENT

In the quiet corners of creation, where the alchemy of words meets the canvas of imagination, this book took its form. It is a testament to all the collective support and efforts of those who contributed to its fruition.

To my muse, whose silent whispers guided the pen and whose inspiration breathed life into these pages, thank you for being the part that ignited the flame of creativity.

To my family, for their understanding during the solitary hours spend crafting these pages.

To my friends, whose conversations and shared experiences added depth and color to the palette of ideas.

To the team, whose support and commitment to excellence has left an indelible mark on these pages.

Lastly to the countless authors, poets, thinkers whose works have shaped my own perspective and fueled the fire of my creativity

Each person mentioned, and those unnamed but not forgotten, has played a vital role in bringing this book to fruition. To all who have touched this project with their presence, encouragement and expertise, thank you for being an integral part of this journey.

PREFACE

Dear readers, welcome to a journey into the realms of thought, emotion and the intricacies of an introverted mind.

These words, carefully penned, are more than ink on paper; they are fragments of contemplation, whisper of thoughts and echoes of the countless moments that shaped my life.

As a writer, my intent is not to dictate, but to share a collection of thoughts, emotions and reflections. It is my hope that these pages resonate with you, offering understanding and companionship.

With gratitude,
Hungchano M Kikon

MEMOIR

The candle flickers and the wind howls
Raindrops and the smell of dirt
Cigarettes with ashes on a tray
An open book with scribbled lines
Potted plants next to empty frames
An instrument with no strings to play
Manuscript with pages to fill
Of confessions of an introvert
With deadlines fixed in an hourglass

*Navigating Love & Heartaches by an
Introvert*

TO FIND PURPOSE

My thoughts are scattered, yet secure and calm
An effort to put together,
A feeling rooted in all places
Wondering into spaces of my own
An attempt at writing, about a feeling that's constantly
changing.
It's a beautiful chaotic mess,
And the only thing that's certain
Is the constant grin on my face
It's the feeling of home, of being together and not alone
For the only things that's assuring is this love with you

CHOOSING YOU

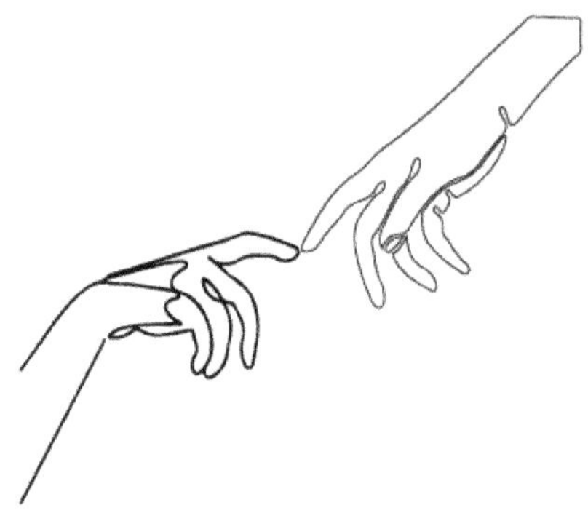

Choosing you and losing you
You fixed me then broke me
You completed me to make me feel incomplete
Saved me just so you can drown me
Took my pain to make me numb
Pulled me close to push me far
Yet I still chose you to lose you

LOSING YOU

The closer I get to you
The further you walk away
Maybe you don't realise
But you are now just a shadow in the distance

LOSING ME

I stayed silent when you roared
I showed grace when you didn't deserve mercy
I absorbed your tears so you could laugh
I blamed myself when you were wrong
I fixed myself when you were broken
I hated me to give you love
I kept losing pieces of me bit by bit
To see you grow not to quit
I gave my all not to let you fall
And you walked out when I had nothing left but to crawl

LOSING US

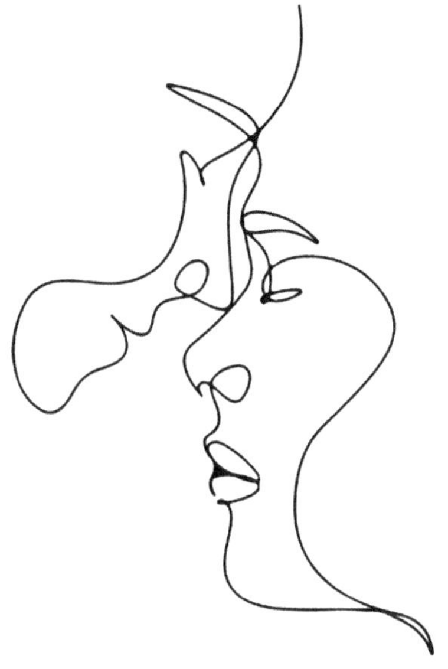

Restrictions with conversations
Losing the spirit of communications
Listening but not really
Just to finish the tallies.
I miss us when we had time
Creating moments on FaceTime,
Isn't it strange?
As we stick to mere exchange,
Of updates in pieces
And not goodnight kisses.

YOU

'You' are a constant reminder
Of the life I left behind
'You' are my home
That swallowed my existence
'You' are my strength
As you watch me fall
'You' are a memory
Of the darkness in the light
'You' are a melody
Of songs I don't sing anymore

ME

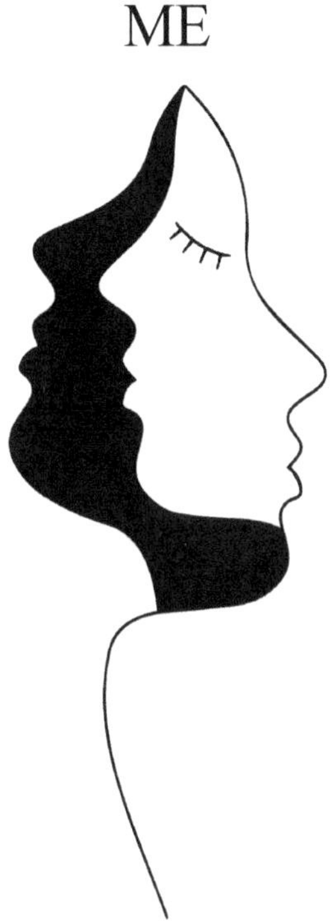

I am trying to create this version of me
One where I seek peace
One where I deny attention
One where my life is not in shambles
A version of me that's Happy
Buoyant and not afraid of solitude
I am creating a version of me
That's all me and not influenced

LESSONS

I am still learning
Learning how to unlove you
Learning how to not be broken
You say you want me back
But where were you when I wanted
How can you love and choose to unlove me?
Is this all a mere game to you?

CHOICES

When you lie down in your empty room
I hope your life feels contented
When you stumble and fall
I hope you have a hand to pick you up
When life seems unbearable
I hope you have a shoulder to lean on
When it gets too quiet
I hope you turn around to a room full of your people
I hope the choices you make
Are your choices for life
And if I do ever cross your mind
I hope you replace me with your other thoughts

3AM

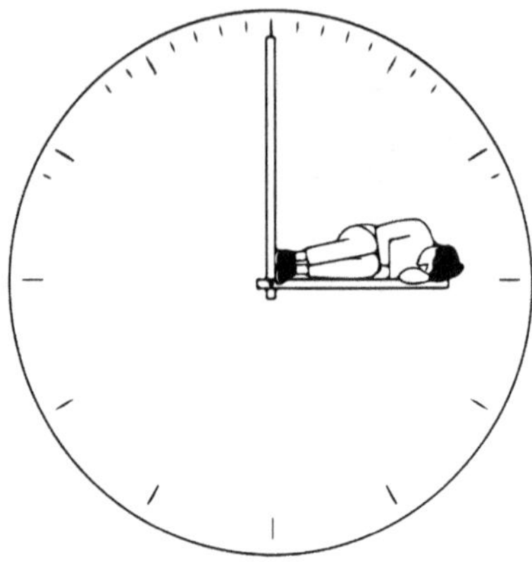

3am with a broken heart
Phone's ringing and a quick restart
Lights flashing in an empty room
A cold bed and the smell of your perfume
Pictures, post its, silence all around
3am with letters on the ground

ALL YOUR LIES

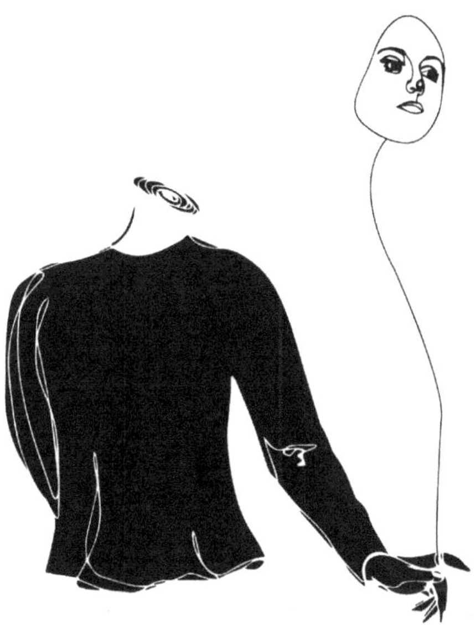

I saw your lies buried behind your tears
Your promises of the only one
Made me wondered if those wasted years
Were all different faces that you'd worn

MY BROKEN HEART

You asked to see me again
But I knew the parts of me would crumble
I would be right back where you left
And though every part of me wanted
A glimpse of you next to me
I would be left again
To repair the damages of my longingness

IT'S OK

I want you to know that it's ok
It's ok if you are tired
It's ok if you feel burned out
It's ok if you want to let me go
All you have to do is say it

FIGHTING A LOSING BATTLE

The promises of constant communication and
understanding
Are now covered by unread messages and unanswered
calls.
Were we fighting a battle that was already lost?
Or did we just pretend to be winning.

TEMPORARY LOVE

I wasn't yours and you weren't mine
Just silent glances and awkward smiles
Our coffee dates and pancakes at nine
Virtual and apart a thousand mile
Short lived like a glass of wine
Kept me hopeful and happy for a while

IF

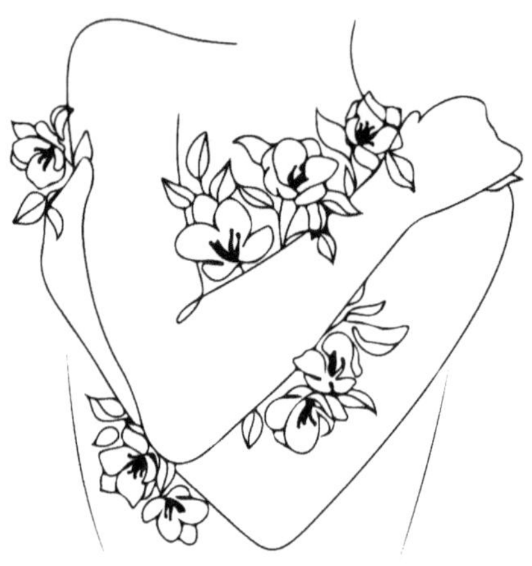

If I just hold on to you a little longer
Maybe I will see you look for me
Maybe I'll hear you call my name
Maybe I'll watch you fall back in love with me
For as long as we could, we did and we made it
But how do we fight a love that's not ours anymore

FAILING LOVE

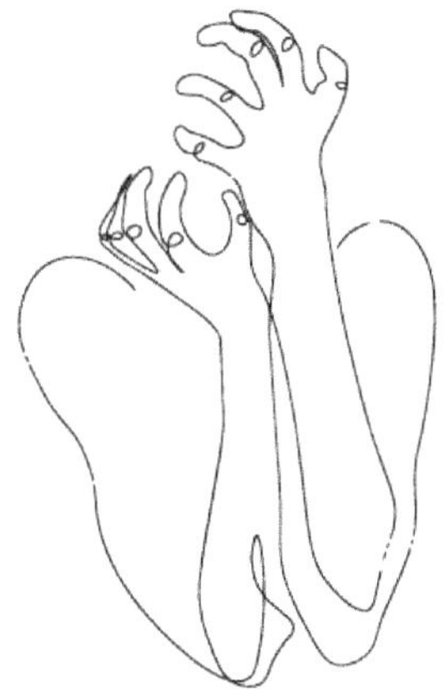

You said you were happy
Felt understood and respected
But the scars you were hiding
Faking it to make it look pretty
Tore down our walls we build so high
Shattered and broke the promise of forever
Now you feel suffocated
Misunderstood and burden with sacrifices
While I stay hidden with guilt

BROKEN

Distance isn't what broke us,
It was the lies, the betrayal, You!

UNWANTED

Love is what you don't want right now,
But Love is all I have to offer

MAYBE

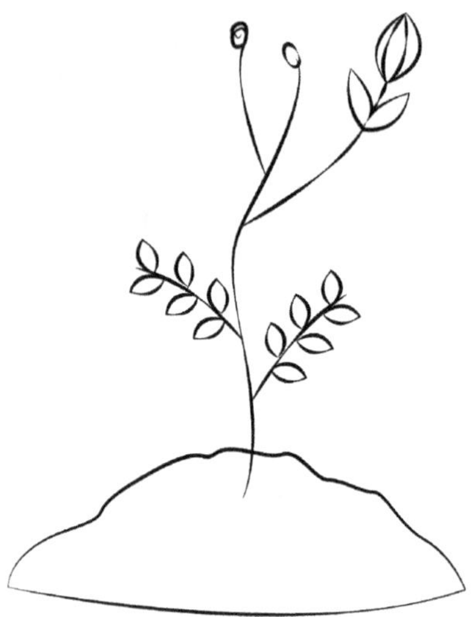

Maybe after all the pain, after all the hurt,
Maybe Dead won't hurt this much

MOVING ON

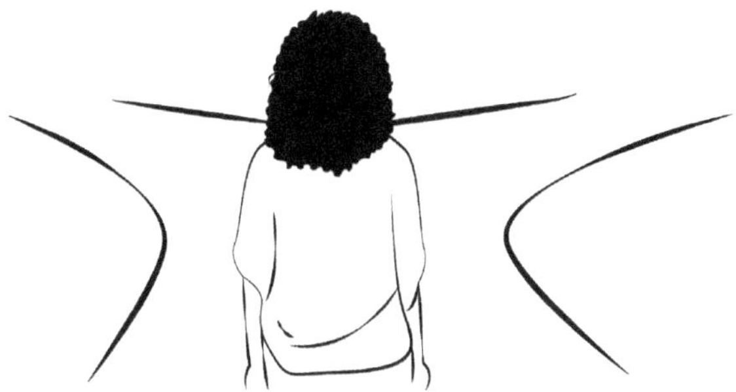

You moved on as though I was just a passenger you chose to drop off
At a stop that's far away from home.
A home you promised was ours
During the journey where the road was yours
Then you made it mine
Made me carve my name
But when came a turn
You moved on with an empty seat
Looking for a new promise on the streets

THE IDEA OF LOVE

I love the idea of love
Falling in love, being in love
But often times, the idea of love
Clouds my judgement of an actual love
And I end up loving so deeply
That I refuse to step back
Even when my heart starts bleeding

DEATH

The hardest thing I ever had to do was to get over you,
But sometimes Life calls for death even when you are
breathing

SILENT SACRIFICE

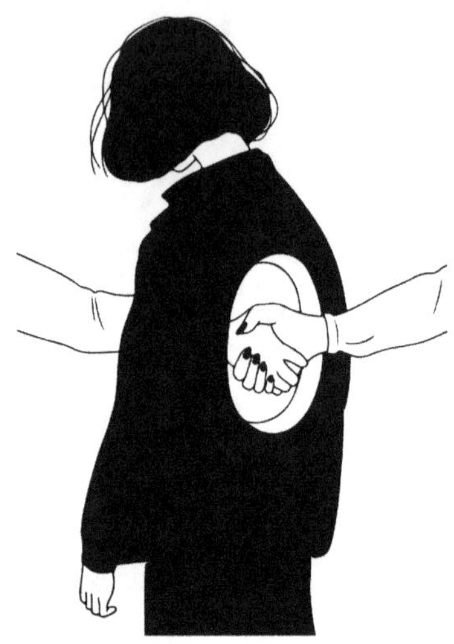

I am removing the part of you that makes you sad and weary
I am choosing to step back so you can walk past me

TO LET YOU GO

I'm letting you go
In a way, I'm letting me go
Turn and walk away
To words that promises you serenity
I'm letting you go
To heal myself from our adventures
To guard my recovery
I'm letting you go
So will you please let me go too?

REFLECTIONS

I am scared of turning you into a person you won't smile at
When you look in the mirror.

An Introvert's Daily Affirmations

WANDERING

My mind is a neighborhood
Of broken glasses on the streets
Of shattered windows on the car
My mind is a playground
Of dying roses and a muddy ground
Of empty swings and rusted slides
My mind is a home
Of locked rooms and half painted walls
Of thousand footprints with scratches on the door
My mind is a mess
Of freckled emotions and peaceful conflicts

OLD SCHOOL LOVE

I am an old school kind of love
I love forehead kisses and lasting letters
I don't ask for much
Just to give me what I'm worth enough
I am silent when I am
But a talker when I can
I don't run away when things get hard
Nor will I watch you fall apart
I'm happy with the tinest effort
And I don't expect you to be an expert
I'm an old school kind of love
One that's true and not unheard of

ENDLESS BEGINNINGS

It's a twisted circle of endless beginnings
One often carved out of pieces that's left
Breaking into smaller messes
Taking away the meaning of what it all started with
And all that remain are the unwanted part
Left for me to make it whole again

ANXIETY

Is this life enough to keep me from running
Am I contented or just caught up by my habits,
Too afraid for changes
The corners of my room seems to get smaller
Or is my mind building its own walls
A feeling I can't seem to outgrow
Pulling me apart slowly in bits and pieces
Gasping for air in an open space
Will I ever be able to break out of my own chains?

ALONE

34

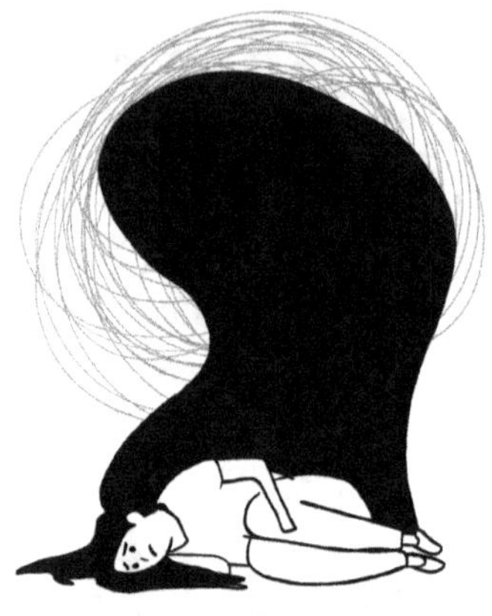

Defined by spaces but confined by barriers
Silent but deafening in nature
It's addictive, to be alone, to feel contented

STREET LAMPS

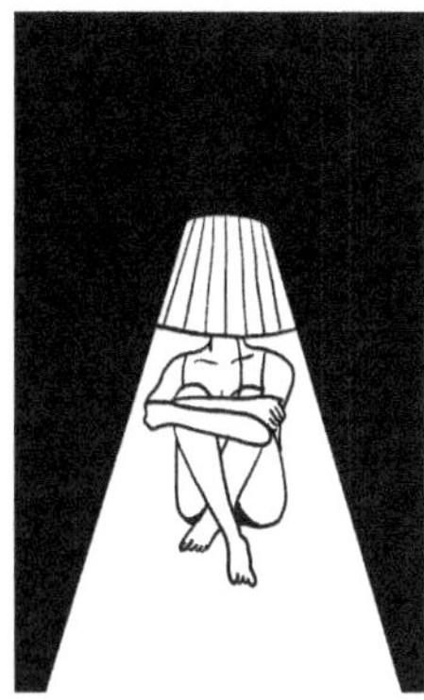

Slowly feeling faded
Disappearing into the distance
I see myself standing but my soul's a hundred steps behind
The street lights on me, the reason I am seen
As I watch myself under those lights,
I see the weight drawing on my shoulders
I see the circles forming underneath my eyes
I feel the heaviness of my sigh.
My breathing is not steady
I have been smoking more than I should
You can tell from my lips.
My skin doesn't wrinkle anymore, guess I haven't smiled
in a long time
My neck looks strained from all the nodding;
I am too tired to speak.
Just a matter of time, then I'll step out of the street lamps
Into the darkness that soothes my soul
The lights too bright for me now
Maybe someday I will come around again.

DOUBTS

I'm starting to see the lines forming
Within the base that we build this on
I can see your doubts and feel your thoughts
Questioning my efforts and my actions
Unsure of the commitment, if it's rather a burden now

WARY

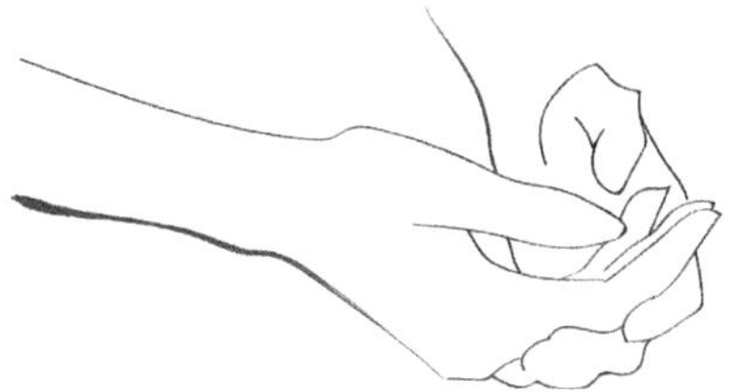

A storm is brewing
Within our souls
With winter here
Our hearts are frosty
Spitting venoms at each other
But none to take the poison out
Counting down the sacrifices
Adding on the disapproval
Watching the days go
Striking out the numbers
But before we grow numb to the pain
Let a Hope linger.

BLANK CANVAS

What looks like a blank canvas
But is actually painted with colors of speculation and void
Silent in nature, to take course on its own accord.
A patient mind, feeling out of place.
An effort to comprehend the reality
It's will to take hold of life's spaces and faces
Of spaces that seem uncertain, in places that feel sane
Will a lie be accurate?
To escape in a form that still leaves the heart feeling
contented?
But if spaces were filled of lies, in places that feel at home
Where'd you go when faces seem distant, and you run out
of places that's constant.
So how do you bargain for a blank canvas?
That's fill with colors not seen to man.

DARKNESS

Colors starts to fade
Darkness starts to set
In our lives that once filled with joy
Now covered Grey
Screaming into nothingness
Too blinded to see the pain
How do we heal another
When we are broken beyond repair
As I lay
My mind recalling
Of words I said, of words I read, of words I heard
I cry myself to sleep
Knowing I'll have to do this again

IT'S OK TO BE SAD

Sadness can be overwhelming at times
Happiness may be at a distance
Heart is wary and time is ticking
This pain feels like an hourglass that's losing
All of its sound but never runs out.
I may be sad, I know, cause it shows
A little broken, a little healing
Once in a while I feel beaten
But I'll be better, of this I'm sure
Just a little pushing and a little hashing
Silently repairing what's left of me
To make the best of what I'll be

ATTENTION

Not all attention comes with good intention

DO YOU….?

Do you ever feel broken but without pain
Do you feel numb even when you move
Does it hurt but still see no scars
None to blame yet none to lean
Feel lonely but still surrounded
Unable to speak yet the tears won't stop
Do you ever try to figure out,
If it's just phases or the end of life
Does being weary makes you weak
Or do you dust and play pretend
I keep searching for answers
But find myself broken yet without pain

DEAD END

To have all the freedom in the world
Yet to not know it's power
To be able to make choices
Yet to not know the options
To have no barriers
But have no control
To have all directions
And not know how to navigate
To ask for more
But unwilling to listen
It's an open road with a dead end.

METAPHOR

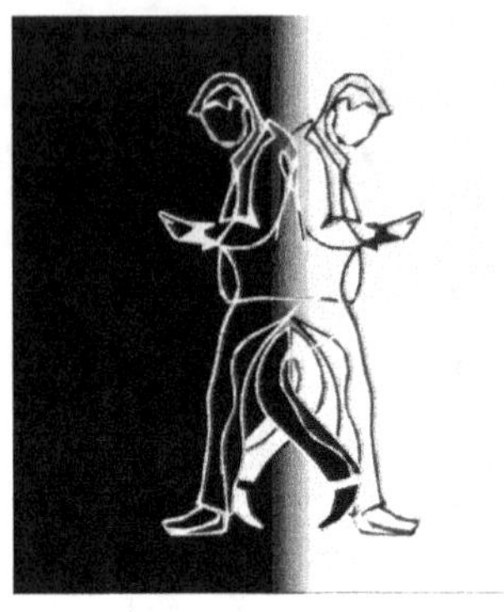

All that people are at the end
Is a metaphor
A symbol of something else
Running away from who we truly are
The world lies buried
With rather more quantity than quality
With demolitions and dominance
Our lives are overshadowed
But this I believe
Life is a gift, be assured
Don't you just let my breath go in vain
For no man will feel my pain
No man will feel my regret
If I let live a wasted life
So, let me live in a world I build
For I am not here to just survive
I am not here just for merry making
Let me fill myself with love
And grace myself with freedom
Let me be here to make my stay worthwhile.

LATE NIGHT RANDOMS

EP 1

It all came back
All the scars and the pain
All the healing went to vain
Just a call from you
And I saw myself drowning in tears.
My heart stopped for a second
Memories of us,
Memories of you
Buried deep were now dug out
Out in the open, all scattered
Nothing at that moment mattered

EP 2

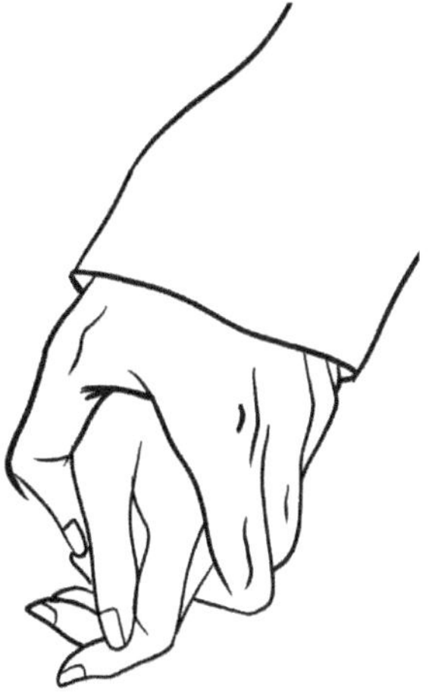

I thought I knew true love
One that stays and never leave
Even when the days get rough
Someone to hold and give.
I thought I had true love
Though it came and went
Each one with promises around
All failed to keep its end.
I still believe in love
To come to me when it had to be
I'll be a little lost and confused
With what, why, if and how
A dying faith and a hope that's fading
Yet I'll hold it when it comes to me

EP 3

It's raining,
Waiting for my thoughts to hit
To give voices to my pain.
It's silent and lonely,
But the craving for a presence is gone.
It's comforting,
To be alone.
It's dark, but the walls are broken.
I'm drenched but alive
Alone, dark, broken…but living

EP 4

I am unable to understand your pain
That you hold so high
I am unable to hear your screams
When you say you are hurt under your breath
How do I help you?
When I see you do all wrong
How can I heal you?
When you cut yourself so deep.
Tell me your stories
I am here to listen,
But you sit and lie for attention
To make me believe your intentions.
I've held my hand out
A hundred, a million times
You push and pull, a game is all.
I am unable to see your good
When you are damage at the roots.

EP 5

Empty spaces felt like home
Met you at a time when you were torn
Saw you put yourself together piece by piece
Watch you grow, then watch you leave

EP 6

Am I worth the fight?
Or are you just stringing me along.

EP 7

You made me believe that my love was enough…
Enough for you till it felt too short

EP 8

Your memories became distant
The thought of you weren't constant
The sound of your voice were fading
And your pictures weren't worth saving
I saw you leave and walk right out
When I needed just a last goodbye
You left with a burden hanging
Running back with problems, begging
But I've filled this house which once was ours
With new sets of pictures and fresh flowers

EP 9

I keep looking for a glimpse of life..
In all places I know is dead.

EP 10

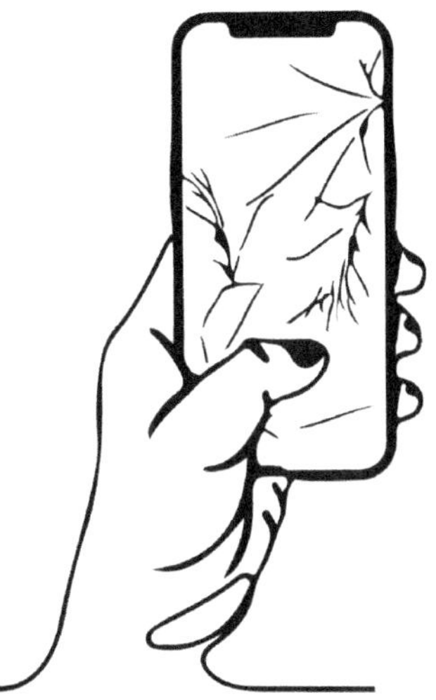

When you lie down in bed at night
Do you think of me?
When your phone screen lights up
Do you hope it's me?
When you close your eyes to sleep
Do you dream of me?
Cause when I lie in bed at night
I cry myself to sleep
When my phone screen lights up
I secretly hope it's you
And when I close my eyes to sleep
My soul stays up the night

EP 11

My life became your stories
As you filled up your tallies
Telling the world of our escapade
Unaware of how fast it escalades
We became a topic of conversation
In faces unknown of our separation
Will time heal these wounds that are cut too deep?
Or will it forever let me weep

EP 12

My Introverted soul
Where everyone feels like a stranger
Unknown faces came to my rescue
When the selected few
Abandoned and pretended

EP 13

A little lost, a little scared
In a world that seem to care
A wounded heart with the biggest smile
Unhappy for a while

M.I.S.O

There were a lot of days where I felt like my soul had given up living inside of me
There were moments of relentless blame unable to see
Times where the whole idea of my existence seemed wasted with paragraphs
I saw myself disappear into darkness, locked into rooms smeared in memories and photographs
Which took me down a rabbit hole of why I shouldn't be here, Breathing…
I saw my warriors, ones that gave life a meaning
Break down doors for me to pull me out
Spend their days on me and left no doubt
Made me believe when my body went numb
All I saw, nothing but a dump
Put living back in me when every inch of me tried to kill every part of me.

But…
I'm grateful for my little crowd
Standing by me, showing my scars so proud
Those cups of coffee and endless conversations,
My mind engaged with no distractions
The silent promises they make in the living room
To laugh at themselves, taking one dig at each other in the bedroom
Dragging me in for a dance at our favourite songs
With two left feet and the steps all wrong
I'm grateful for my little crowd
Who chose me despite my dark cloud.